Miscellaneous Wreckage

Books by the same author

The Moon Road (chapbook, 2001)

What the Wound Remembers (1993)

The Possibilities of Chinese Trout (1986)

Disturbances (1981)

Miscellaneous Wreckage

Greg Simison

thistledown press

Thistledown Press Ltd.
410 2nd Avenue North
Saskatoon, Saskatchewan, S7K 2C3
www.thistledownpress.com

Library and Archives Canada Cataloguing in Publication

Simison, Greg, 1946–, author
Miscellaneous wreckage / Greg Simison.
Poems.
ISBN 978-1-927068-86-1 (pbk.)
I. Title.
PS8587.I313M58 2014 C811'.54 C2014-905353-3

Cover and book design by Jackie Forrie
Printed and bound in Canada

Canada Council for the Arts Conseil des Arts du Canada

Saskatchewan Arts Board

Canadian Heritage Patrimoine canadien

Thistledown Press gratefully acknowledges the financial assistance of the Canada Council for the Arts, the Saskatchewan Arts Board, and the Government of Canada through the Canada Book Fund for its publishing program.

Acknowledgements

Earlier versions of some of these poems have previously been published in the following periodicals, e-magazines, and anthologies: *Crannóg, FreeFall Magazine,The Pine Beetle Review,The Greenboathouse Reader,Yearbook of American Poetry,Rocksalt (An Anthology of Contemporary B.C. Poetry).The Society,blue skies poetry.*

Many thanks to friends and fellow writers who read and commented on the poems found in this book; in particular, John Lent, Brian Armstrong, and Angie Abdou. And, of course, love to my daughter, Sarah, for her fanatical support, and my son, Alex, who has finally forgiven me for not writing like Charles Bukowski. A tip of the tea cosy to my brother, Rick, who opens his island hideaway to me for several months a year, and Darlene Wright for her camera work and cemetery cruising. Finally, thank you to Robert Currie, Donna Lee Howes, Sarah Simison, and all of those involved in the Saskatchewan Festival of Words for making me feel at home in Moose Jaw.

Contents

in memory of

old friends too soon gone

Jim Hood, Rick Johnston, and Ian Magee

Male Enhancement

Go ahead,
flip through the book, but
you might first glance around
to make sure no one is watching.

Come on,
be brave, scan a poem
or a least a stanza or two.
I promise your penis won't fall off.

Oh, granted,
it may shrink a little,
but remember, when you're hung
as well as we are, who's going to notice?

Besides, it's
well worth the tiny loss
considering the guaranteed huge
increase in the size of your sensitivity,

and it's a well-known fact
that no woman can resist
a man who possesses a big
sensitivity, and knows how to use it.

Kootenay Lake

This lake seldom surrenders its dead —
glacier fed, as cold in pockets as the North Atlantic,
only mild surprise would greet the arrival of an iceberg
in the bay at Kaslo one morning.

Clumsy fishermen, broken prospectors,
deck hands blown from sternwheelers, drift
perfectly preserved among thousand-year old trees,
sinking slowly as they turn to stone,

eventually joining other legends —
trout, as long as a liar can spread his arms,
sturgeon that swam with dinosaurs, drowned mammoths:
prehistoric deadheads, as fresh

as any lifted from permafrost.
Accept these as possible, then anything is possible —
living dragons, sasquatch roaming the steep shoreline,
ghost ships plying night waters.

'The stuff of poets and barflies,' some scoff,
insisting a sudden glimmer in the depths
is just a lost fishing lure, or play of light on broken glass,
anything but a watch chain dangling

from an old-fashioned vest,
or the glint in a frozen eye. But no matter on which side
of the argument they fall, cold or superstition restrict swimmers
to the warmer shallows,

keep older, wiser fishermen
trolling the lake's thin skin. The deeps, the preserve
of foolhardy night-lampers unaware of what grim catches
rise to their small bobbing moons.

Funerals

I always assume there's been a mistake,
a small typo on the pickup sheet —

the wrong house number, Rose instead
of Ross Street, Simpson instead of Simison —

sit nervously through the eulogies
anticipating a long, bony finger tapping me

on the shoulder, the rustling of papers
as a clipboard is double-checked, the gentle

lifting of a puzzled corpse from the casket,
and an apologetic voice whispering in my ear,

Sorry to interrupt, but . . .

Observer

At 86, his sight failing, he's
put away his telescope and

tattered astronomical charts.
And though the names and

co-ordinates of his celestial
favourites are now vanishing

into the ether along with every-
thing else, some nights an old

curiosity, briefly rejuvenated,
steers him onto the back lawn

and lifts his eyes to a darker
sky where, one by one, the

last of his stars burn out.

Flock Mentality

With the fine for feeding wildlife
now topping two-hundred dollars,
my neighbour patrols his yard,
wildly waving his greasy red cap,
scattering a dozen mallards from
his lawn onto the road where,
like water meeting an obstruction,
they surge around him and back onto the grass.

I wish him luck and lots of time.
With its long history of fine dining,
that lawn is a culinary legend, a neon
green beacon pinpointing JOE'S PLACE,
as firmly fixed in mallard memory as the
seasonal shift of the sun off their wingtips,
as enduring as the Pole Star steering their tiny
one-track brains from handout to handout across the planet.

Dementia 1

Only three days
home from the hospital
and, despite his promises,
already he's uncooperative;

struggling with everyone,
pushing the insulin needle away,
spitting out his six pills, twice a day.

And how appropriate he's back
to eating like a sparrow. A trapped bird,
his frantic eyes fly to the corners of the room,

desperate for a way out
                    he once knew.

Dementia 2

When the care-worker arrives to perform
a mental assessment, my father turns on the charm,
flirting with her in a manner only old men can get away with.

Dazzling her with rare clarity and wit,
he adopts the role of a lovable, orphaned Oliver,
who, as soon as she's gone, reverts to The Artful Dodger,

smirking, and smoothly slipping
her inflated evaluation of him beneath his coat;
a pocket-watch or silk handkerchief 's worth of credit;

swag with which he'll buy a few more
months of freedom, having relegated the rest
of us to vile conspirators, huddled around the kitchen table,

all heartless Bill Sikes and Fagins.

How the English Die

If there's a single word that best describes her,
then *proper* would be perfect. In all those years
I never once witnessed even a minor slip in manners,
or the slightest quiver of that stiff, upper lip.

I've even heard how, near the end, she apologized
to the nurse holding her hand for any inconvenience
she might have caused, and don't doubt that, had she lived
another day, she'd have sent flowers, and an appropriate card.

Cape Horn

We always stop on that steep
mountainside halfway through
the journey, and halfway to the stars.

Perched on that lookout,
500 feet above Slocan Lake,
we once again attempt to take it in,

absorb that massive landscape
before turning away, as always,
considerably smaller than we arrived,

suspecting that if we lingered
too often, or too long, we might
disappear completely, our old Buick

joining the rusting cars of vanished
tourists littering the shoulders along
Highway 6 for miles in either direction.

Winter Fishing, Kootenay Lake

On these big lakes the local fishing boats boast heaters,
wool-lined squall jackets, thermoses of coffee laced with rum,

but, once you can see your breath, floatation devices are
stowed below, joining the other warm-weather gear, all useless

when the wind turns vicious. Capsize at this time of year and
no life jacket, rabbit's foot, caul, or other charm will save you.

You could try prayer, but better make it loud. Like anyone
else here with half-a-brain, God heads south with Thanksgiving.

Fishing Okanagan

Throughout July we chased them deeper.
Now, well into a dry August, finally resorting to
downriggers, our tension mirrors that of the filament.

Here blind hooks hunt regions in excess
of a hundred feet. In that black realm where the
thin line between fact and fiction starts to dissolve

we troll for legends.

Travel Insurance

Today my daughter
flies from Regina to Ottawa,

and despite the claim
that you're more likely

to die in a car accident
on the way to the airport,

whenever my children fly
I spend the day with fingers

and toes tightly crossed,
hoping for clear skies, a new aircraft,

and a pilot whose wife
was oh-so-good-to-him last night,

and promises to be again
the moment he arrives safely home.

Floor Play

In the den I glance up from the page
to catch her dancing across the living room.

Soon the book is down and my toes are up,
tapping out the beat of the waltz, wondering

if she's content to dance alone, or does she
imagine some ideal lover, some light-footed

Casanova holding her in his arms. And
isn't that the usual male reaction, to assume

it's a lover she desires and not simply
solitude, or just some damn good dancer.

Though, if it's the latter, I'd be of little help,
being the only man so hopelessly uncoordinated

he was drummed-out of the Arthur Murray
Dance Studio. But tonight, for just one minute,

I wish I could swap these two left feet for
Fred Astaire's, and one sweet turn around the room.

Feast

Though usually indiscriminate raiders
of valley gardens, fruit trees, and black-
berry slopes, the bears shun this ancient,
twisted apple tree beside the road. All winter
unmauled offerings sway from its branches,

the sourness so legendary even the earth
refuses its windfalls. But for us, colour-
starved in a white season, it offers a sweet
and generous gift, kindly keeping, beneath
their lids of snow, its small green lanterns lit.

Ex-Wife

Ever considerate, at my request she
spends her Saturday searching a local
Victoria cemetery to find and photograph
the graves of paternal grandparents I never
knew, then, noting how young they died, enquires
after my health, asking if I ever did complete that Last
Will and Testament gathering dust on a corner of my desk.

Ever opportunistic, with a reputation
for uncanny accuracy when it comes to
premonitions, she triggers goose bumps,
has me checking my tongue in the mirror before
desperately booking that annual physical I've been
putting off for five years, while she, her day made, strolls
in the warm, west coast sun, the picture of perfect health.

Dress Parade

Well into his eighties, it's not simply
a matter of the old Sergeant Major stubbornly
clinging to life, but more a case of whoever controls
his next posting wanting to prepare things properly.

On some massive parade square in the
afterlife, millions of souls shuffle their gleaming
boots and nervously tug at their tunics, awaiting the
arrival of the one man to whom even the gods defer.

Ainsworth Cemetery

With nothing but a wagon track
climbing the high ridge to the cemetery,

the dead count on the good will and strong
shoulders of friends and family to hoist them

halfway to heaven, then pray shaky credit for a
few good deeds carries them the rest of the way.

Losing It

I misplaced it this morning — one word.
I'm told such losses are to be expected in middle age
but they should be found in five, or, on a bad day, ten seconds.

I groped for this one a full fifteen minutes
before giving up, only to stumble over it hours later
when I carelessly dropped a cigarette in my lap: 'Cremation.'

A simple enough word. I can
see losing ligularia or discombobulated, perhaps
struggling momentarily to nudge frangible or diaphanous

from the brain to the tongue. But cremation?
What's next? Common objects? Places? Of course, once I'd
found cremation I had no idea why I wanted it in the first place.

On the upside — from what I can recall I've
always been an optimist — maybe whatever's working
its way through my aging brain, barring doors to storage rooms

that once swung freely, will eventually
forever lock away my past, and perhaps that's not
such a terrifying prospect. Perhaps somewhere in the future

I'll run into one of the few women
I've ever loved to find her memories equally imprisoned,
and I can start reliving those nights of frenzied passion

with good old . . . what's-her-name.
That's assuming one of us remembers what comes
after the last piece of clothing whispers its way to the floor.

Hiking at Sixty

Ignoring the younger risk takers,
two turkey vultures play the odds
and slowly circle the seniors' trail.

We two old men, the day's best bet.

V

Five months severely
tests the memories of geese.

Twice a year they take
to the air practicing formation

flying, relearning the
ancient alphabet of migration.

Working their way
through ragged *A*s, *E*s, and *Y*s,

they finally abandon
vowels in favour of consonants,

eventually scrawling
childish, shaky *V*s across the sky:

the long wavering hooks
they'll hitch to the meridians

to guide them safely
from one summer to another.

Over Dinner We Discussed Killing the Rat

What you're never told when you buy these fluff balls is,
should they survive the first few weeks of constant fondling
and heart-stopping plunges to the floor, cancer invariable
claims them before their third birthday. For months
we've watched ours deteriorate: tumour-laden,
blind in the left eye, gimp-footed in old cedar shavings,
now more Quasimodo than Mickey Mouse.

Over dessert, having eliminated expensive vets, whirlpool
tours of the sewage system, and 'bashing head against a wall'
— I mustn't put off getting the boy counselling much longer —
we settle on a favourite treat laced with sleeping pills.
Middle-aged, my own health questionable, all evening I've tried
to shake-off doubts about the wisdom of setting such a precedent
while the rat's remaining eye nails mine with a last sleepy wink.

Justice

It is with great satisfaction
and no guilt whatsoever that
I learn the priest who terrified
me at twelve with dire warnings
about the dangers of masturbation
has recently himself gone blind.

Holiday Shots

He poses on a sand dune, the Pyramids
of Giza rising from the desert behind him. Astride the
Great Wall of China he stares west as though anticipating
the arrival of Mongols, waves goodbye in France
before vanishing into the caves at Lascaux.

Meanwhile, north of Crestwynd, I circle a collapsing
farmhouse abandoned in a wheatfield like an old skull;
its rusty cans, broken tools and flattened sheds add
their whispers to ancient tent rings and lost arrow heads,
quietly insisting on an equal place in history.

Dreams of the Grand Banks

Amateur anthropologists, we sift
through rock mounds in the field looking
for artefacts: pounders, scrapers, awls
and spear points, gathered and tossed here,
broken and twisted beyond any use, alongside
all the miscellaneous wreckage of farm life.

And though no stone tools reveal
themselves, digging through the third pile
we soon expose the old, disjointed bones of
a man's life: a dozen Johnnie Walker bottles,
evidence of a love of whiskey; the rusted cans of
Repeater, his tobacco brand, and what we first take

to be an old shed roof, on closer
inspection, turns out to be the bleached
ribs of a homemade rowboat. So this strange
country delivers yet one more mystery:
a boat in the middle of a wheatfield. The closest
lake, three miles to the north, alkaline and lifeless

since the last ice age; the closest fish,
ten miles to the west, unless we count the
bony few swimming through rock fifty feet
beneath the ground where he himself now floats.
Of course, ever the romantic, I start reconstructing
a dreamer: a homesick fisherman, new immigrant

or hopeful maritimer with a one-way
ticket, swapping one sea for another, only to
find himself marooned, a landlocked homesteader
with no way back when the dream finally turned
to dust. And I imagine him out there late at
night, seated in the stranded boat, washed up on that

stone island, sipping whiskey and
drunkenly arguing with the indifferent
moon. Rolling one-handed smokes in the
dark, he lights the wooden matches with a
blackened thumbnail, creating sudden small stars,
but stars too brief and too late to steer an old sailor home.

9C

After they took his leg to slow down the
cancer, I visited one evening and announced

he may as well have had a sex change
because from then on I'd be calling him Peggy.

He retaliated in a hoarse whisper
that despite the fact I was God's own fool,

he was still prepared to cut me
a deal on a barely worn right shoe,

but quickly changed the subject, knowing
within a month I'd have the pair for nothing.

Arrangements

With the sudden death of her mother-in-law
still fresh, during a weekend visit my daughter
asks what my wishes are when it's my turn to go.
After confiding my first wish would be that I not
go at all, I express my preferences, ranging from
using my sorry carcass as fish bait, to placing me

on a mountaintop as a well-aged treat for ravens
who, it is rumoured, are not terribly picky eaters.
Always one for compromise, eventually I agree
to cremation and the scattering of my ashes in a
favourite wilderness area, only on the condition the
location never be revealed. No sense importing

the crowd-control problems of Mecca and Jerusalem.

Trigger

This evening
hard evidence
one custom
of the old west
still survives
when halfway
through the
poetry reading
a cell phone
rings
disturbing
the peace
and
thirty hands
lunge for
the holsters
on their hips.

Happy Returns

In order to seat twelve,
the waitress pulls three tables together
and, though placed at the head of them all,

for the most part he's ignored,
left to sit there in that ridiculous T-shirt
(World's Greatest Grampa) listening to their

inane conversations, the resumption
of decade-old feuds, fresh spats, all to the
tune of wailing, snotty-nosed grandchildren.

And he's probably wishing this year's gift
was a second shot at that train he missed
the night she confessed she was pregnant.

Tradition

Working long-handled brushes and wearing
orange, city-issued coveralls and rubber gloves,
they scrub the walls of downtown buildings
they've been caught using as blank canvases.

With bleach and paint remover, and
good old Protestant-work-ethic elbow grease,
they erase gang tags, badly spelled epithets
and brilliant caricatures of friends and enemies.

Terrorists in the war against beige
and Chamber of Commerce approved pastels,
they whitewash brick to appease public outrage
while already planning tomorrow's fresh offences.

And I've long suspected they know
what archaeologists learned long ago, exposing,
inch by inch, the graffiti-covered walls
of Pompeii, Herculaneum, and Capernaum:

that these five, smirking penitents are
proud descendants of the hands that scrawled
CASSIA SECUNDA PUTS OUT,
CENTURIANS SUCK, and FUCK CAESAR.

Visions: Writing on Stone

He never believed in ghosts until
he spent a long, cold night alone
curled beneath a hoodoo on the
north bank of the Milk River

where his dreams were filled with
broken chants, the distant clatter
of pony hooves on sandstone, and
an approaching thunderstorm that

poured buffalo back onto the plains.

Silence

There are no coffee houses left in this town where
one can read in peace or share whispered intimacies.

Now it's all loud music, live or piped-in, demanding
conversations be held at the highest decibel level;

coffee-break chat-fests for loud secretaries and scruffy
philosophers raging over conspiracy theories and espresso.

Give me back the quiet havens that enforced library rules,
hired staff drawn from the ranks of mutes and unemployed

mimes, who'd signal slurpers and enthusiastic babblers
to remove themselves silently, and right bloody now,

while the rest of us glare over lowered books
and ever, ever so quietly, click our atrophied tongues.

Calls

My brother calls at 1 a.m.
to tell me the ambulance has
taken her to the Civic Hospital,

suggests it would be best
if I flew out as soon as possible.
I call my children with the news.

Book a ticket. Pack a suitcase.
With terrible practicality, learned
at her side, include a black suit. A tie.

And realize, on perhaps
this longest night of our lives,
we're all simply small children

who've only been outside
playing grownups until our
mothers call us home, one last time.

Attire

I honour crows and ravens,
properly dressed year round
for either death, or dining out.

It's their haughtiness; the way
they stare down aristocratic beaks
at the bright, migratory riff-raff

that flit from branch to branch
during their stopovers, like package
tourists, giddy, in cheap Hawaiian shirts.

For An Old Lover

According to what I've read,
half the weight of my five-year-old pillow
is accounted for by living and dead dust mites.

And you once predicted I'd spend my life sleeping alone.

Celestial Mechanics

In the same manner that a small
erratic body entering a 'closed system'
influences all calculations, demanding
a revised mathematics, all evening you've
established your orbit while unbalancing my
own, drawing me in as gently, and relentlessly,
as the soft tug of the moon on water's helpless skin.

I Only Wish

Helping fold my laundry,
my daughter pulls a pair of
women's thongs from the basket.

Proclaiming my innocence,
I point out that a dozen
apartments share the laundry room,

that anyone could have forgotten
them in the dryer, while she stares
at me like a cop weighing a bad alibi.

When she spreads the news,
my son, dateless for months, will call,
his voice filled with such unprecedented

awe and respect,
I won't have the heart
to disillusion him with the truth.

A Short History of Wrong Numbers

Most of them are older men
looking for various Simpsons.
Phone books spread on their laps,
their failing eyes misread the 'i' in
the middle of my name for a 'p', or
they're simply clumsy: blunt fingers like
hammers on the tiny buttons of new phones.

"It's Bill from Drinkwater," kept it
short, quickly realizing his mistake
and ending with a curt, "Sorry." Norm,
who it turned out lived in the village of
Lardeau in the heart of Kootenay country,
after his initial, "Moose Jaw! I wanted Dave
in Wynyard!" as though I was at fault for answering

a phone in Moose Jaw when I
wasn't Dave in Wynyard, saw it as
an opportunity to swap local weather
reports and, learning the temperature
here hovered around minus thirty, questioned
the sanity of prairie people. But my all time favourite,
attempting to call another farmer miles south of where I lay sleeping,

was Chuck from Elbow, stuck
in his cow barn at 3 a.m., awaiting
what he "Strongly suspects might be a
goddam breach birth," and who, in ten
informative minutes taught me everything I'll
ever need to know about the apparently self-induced
gynaecological complications of "Bloody, bone-headed bovines!"
He can wake me again, anytime.

Manners

At one time it would have been enough
to have had my mother reaching for the wooden spoon,
watching me wolf down huge servings
of Stephen King, Irving, Wolfe, and James Lee Burke.

But watching me sit down to poetry
would have made her proud, seeing how I savour each
small bite of Stafford, Heaney, Collins
and Kooser. Chewing each morsel thirty-two times,

then thirty-two times again.

Son

in memory of Charlie Wright

Late one night the subject of grief came up,
and he told me how they'd lost a son, stillborn.
How he'd walked the hospital corridors until
he found the doctor, and demanded to see the boy
or, despite his bantam-rooster size, he'd do enough damage
to require a team of surgeons to put things right.

Led to a small anteroom, he was shown the body.
For half an hour he cradled the blue baby in his arms
quietly describing to him all the things that might have been,
then, setting his boy down, he turned, and, never looking back,
walked out to the parking lot and the long drive home
to that house filled with perfect daughters.

In Transit

All morning
I track his progress on the clock:
ninety minutes to Swift Current, two more
hours to Medicine Hat, another two to Lethbridge.

My eyes, shifting
from the clock face to the TV,
see that death is far too busy with
a train wreck in Quebec, a head-on collision in Manitoba,

to bother with small stuff
like my son making his way home
this Monday morning, and I hope, as
usual, ignoring my advice to drive with care.

Put it to the floor, boy,
before that reaper, harvesting souls in a
ditch near Brandon, discovers he's one short
of his quota and turns his attention further west.

Preserves

Years ago
he licked the sweet syrup
from her fingers whenever
she canned fruit: the shelved jars
of summer that warmed their Januaries.

This morning,
retrieving the last of his
boxes exiled to the damp cellar,
how appropriate to find her hunched over
the stove, wrapped in a sour steam, pickling beets.

Grim, and bloody to the elbows.

Before She Needed Hearing Aids

I once made the mistake of saying
within earshot of my ex-wife, that
writing poetry was better than sex.

She interrupted, claiming that was
only because writing a poem lasted
somewhat longer than two minutes.

Of course,
I'd only meant sex with her.

Mortality Table

The latest insurance statistics
informed me I may live another
fifteen years. Time for perhaps
three or four more books, one last
love affair, and, following form,
a final messy separation.

And I was left feeling quite cocky
until an asterisk dragged my finger
to the bottom of the page where I
was instructed to subtract three years
for every ten a smoker, four if also a drinker,
and an additional decade for choosing

to live alone. Though momentarily
staggered by the drastically reduced
lifespan, I soon recovered as I lovingly
stared into my full-length mirror, impressed
with how remarkably good I look for what
the Canadian Insurance Corporation insists

is a very old corpse.

Westerly

After months of fighting the prevailing winds,
newcomers eventually earn their sea legs.

Anticipating sudden gusts, they learn the knack
of constantly shifting their centre of gravity,

a skill that keeps them upright, but still reeling
like drunken sailors. Even in death there's no relief:

in the cemeteries all the headstones lean
a fraction more to the east every year.

Weathered marble and granite sails
slowly ferry the dead to Manitoba.

Indian Summer

Two weeks into November
and high-temperature records
are broken almost every afternoon.
But that hot stretch of blue is a trap.

The last wedge of geese
passed overhead a week ago,
but I've yet to see any bet their lives
on this late heat wave by returning north.

And, though a newcomer,
I'm not so foolish as to dig out
the shorts and sandals packed away
weeks ago, always keeping in mind the words

of an old farmer overheard on
Coffee Row: *Never gamble with winter.*
Just pull on yer Stanfields in September
and chip 'em off in May.

Tick

I'm told to wait
until we're back at the farm-
house before attempting to remove it;

told the cure
is to bathe it in alcohol
and it will release its grip soon enough.

They must think me
a complete fool. I've been to these
farm parties before and know that once

free alcohol appears
there's no stopping the thirsty bastards
until the host is drained completely dry.

Rhea Ranch

The Velociraptor's foot has travelled
seventy-five million years to reappear
at the ends of those thick, scaly legs,
lifting the rheas exactly high enough
to meet me eye to black, bottomless eye.

Evolved from the earliest species
believed to have possessed feathers,
doubts regarding the impossible leap
from dinosaur to bird soon vanished as
we strolled through the enclosure,

the broomstick he handed me as we
entered gripped tightly in my sweaty fist. "Just
give em' a whack if they get aggressive,"
he said. "And keep your left hand over your
balls. Those claws can open you with one swipe."

When he saw my envious look
at the passive flock in the next pen over
where his wife, unarmed, carried in feed, he
told me *they* we all males, that if we entered
they'd attack as soon as they scented our testosterone.

Catching us looking, the wife smiled,
waved, and twenty malevolent heads
swivelled in our direction, sifting the air,
glaring just long enough to confirm his warning
before turning back to escort their goddess to dinner.

Turkey Vulture

A biological gaff. Lizard grafted to bird.
A naked, red, wrinkled head. A nose for death.

A downwind stench. But a compensating beauty
in flight — those perfect waltzes with wind shear

and updraft, near stalls and sudden swoops —
leaving hawks and ospreys grounded with envy,

wallflowers at the dance.

Moose Jaw

When I learn of distant acquaintances diagnosed
with cancer, Alzheimer's or heart disease, I
give thanks for living in a place the rest of the world
believes exists only in fiction, just another name belonging
to a long list including Gotham City, Rivendell, and, more
appropriate to this particular region, the village of Dog River.

Of course, there's no guarantee, and it may be seen as
a desperate lunge for the flimsiest of straws, but I
suspect the Grim Reaper is no more intelligent than the
average college graduate who never bothered with a non-requisite
geography course and, reading my address, will only react with an
appreciative chuckle before skipping to the next name on the list.

Neighbours

The couple next door fill my nights
with loud words. Emphatic fists smack
tables and bruise walls, but not yet flesh.

By day they care for disabled children,
lovingly lift and carry those small bundles
of twisted bones with such unexpected gentleness

I grudgingly forgive them my interrupted dreams.

Barista

She talked me into a dark blend
rather than my usual medium;
informed me it was a premium organic coffee,
then, leaning closer, gushed,
Like this is absolutely my favourite.
The taste reminds me of the smell
of fresh rain on a summer evening.
I smiled, and escaped as quickly as possible.

Carrying my steaming mug of
organic fresh rain to a patio table,
I was jostled by two men rushing in,
their coveralls identifying them
as Human Resources Division,
Hallmark Greeting Card Corporation —
watched them hustle her out the door,
toss her into a company van, and roar off.

The smell of their exhaust reminded me of standing
downwind from a Tar Sand discharge-water pond,
knee-deep in a golden field of gentle coughing barley.

Nelson, 1992

for Alex

His small-boy dreams
dwarfed Elephant Mountain as
hand-in-hand we walked the streets
where he picked out homes that, short
of winning the lottery, we could never hope to own.

Eliminated thinly-treed lots
on the grounds they couldn't
support windy forts, and renovated
his top choices, creating a young boy's perfect
bedroom and, ever thoughtful, a large bright studio for me.

Back on the highway we found
a Dairy Queen and promptly blew
nearly half our assets on large chocolate
shakes and fries. "Oh well," he said, digging in,
"there goes the swimming pool we have no place for."

Sometimes a Good Meal . . .

Another thin bachelor,
my son emulates me, cooks
dinner for one: charred pork chops,
a half-baked potato, a tin of grey peas,

then dreams all night
of Hollywood starlets, each
one a satin-aproned nymphomaniac,
and hotter in the kitchen than Julia Child.

Salt Spring Island

It's the afterlife, paradise
for successful writers and
retired CBC hosts, the symbol
of finally making it in this country.

While the rest of us plug away,
weighing pathetic royalty cheques
against impossible property values,
tattered ferry schedules in all our pockets.

13 Years On

You haven't missed much.
A dozen wars have sent a million more
lives down the same bullet hole you chose.
Your ex-wives are looking well, content at last
in the arms of other men. And when old friends gather
you still manage to monopolize the conversation.

As we both suspected
growing old is a miserable business you've
neatly sidestepped. No, you really haven't missed
much at all. Except, perhaps, for last night, and
that full moon slowly pulling itself up and over
the Purcell Range to chase its reflection across the lake.

Best Day

For others it might be
that first night with a lover,
a last family reunion, or simply
a day spent fishing a favourite lake.

For me it would be one of
those long Saturday night runs
in that battered old Bel Air toward
some distant barn dance, a case of beer

singing on the back seat,
the windshield pulling us over fresh
horizons filled with the promise of new
girls and all the foolish optimism of seventeen.

Lake Diefenbaker

Two world-record rainbows were
pulled from these waters last year.

The locals insist there are even
bigger ones, cruising like heavily-

armed submarines, shouldering
aside duckweed, their long shadows

dwarfing sandbars. As much an
old sceptic as old fisherman, strolling

the shoreline late in the evening,
I muse on the drunken bragging that by

closing time reduced great whites
to little more than Saskatchewan bait,

all the while attempting to ignore
the distant splashing of what sounds

like small islands leaping in the
dark, and recall, at the Legion, counting

considerably more missing fingers
not wrapped around beer glasses than

can be accounted for by clumsy farmers
caught dreaming of Sundays on the lake.

Death Comes to Saskatchewan

In the mountains he arrives suddenly:
a slab of rock drops from the bluffs north of
Coffee Creek making you one with the cab of your truck.

Or a mudslide or avalanche, sounding
like an approaching train, sweeps you from its
track. With luck your body resurfaces late in the summer.

Or you reach to change radio stations
at the wrong curve on Highway 6, and plunge
five-hundred long feet to the black surface of Slocan lake.

But here you have a chance, five or ten
minutes' grace to make your peace, time to fire
a few feeble, long overdue apologies into the never-ending blue,

while he strides across the fields,
straight for your place, grain parting like the seas,
his cowl and cloak billowing behind him in a bone-rattling wind.

When Good Dates Turn Bad

At dinner she announces
her doctor has placed her
on a daily dose of testosterone,

the latest theory being
it boosts the waning libido
in post-menopausal women.

She then chugs her beer,
insists on arm-wrestling
me for the bill, and smacks

the waitress on the ass
on our way out the door
toward what promises to be

the evening's confusing conclusion.

Wild Blue Yonder

As one wag has observed, my legs now contain
enough titanium to build an ultra-light aircraft.
An appropriate image considering the car accident marked
my first solo flight, and, though impressive in its speed
and distance, witnesses agreed the landing needed work.

Judging from their recent behaviour, my legs now
consider a career in aviation a definite possibility.
Unlike the arms which thrash about like crazed delinquents,
spilling coffee, dropping tools, knocking objects from tables,
the legs are normally the stablest limbs, the most grounded.

But since that first taste of a future not limited
to dragging my aging body from grocery store to library,
escorting my failing bladder from bed to bathroom six times
a night, they've displayed a tendency to fly off
in different directions, test their wings, try their metal.

What will happen when, like the Wright brothers,
they stop squabbling and learn the power of co-operation,
eventually managing to synchronize their spastic contractions?
Imagine the sleepless nights as they take over the house,
perusing weather charts and books on celestial navigation.

How long until the day, slowly struggling up the
post office steps, they decide they've had enough and start
flapping in unison, rising with each kick until I flip upside down,
spread-legged and screaming, a human helicopter, gradually
gaining altitude, turning, and climbing toward the sun?

And that will be it for me, condemned to simply tag along
as they have for sixty years, a reluctant passenger, bag boy
on a long flight to visit geography's famous lower limbs, the ones
that made it really big: the heel of Italy, the foot of the Himalayas,
and, of course, New Zealand's renowned leg of lamb.

By the Styx

Once, sailors wore gold rings in their ears
to pay the burial expenses should they die
in a foreign land, and a small gold coin dangling
from a neck chain covered the ferryman's toll
for that final short voyage.

Earning considerably less than sailors,
we shyly pass him Odes to Death instead
of cash, hoping he has editorial ambitions,
though I suspect that the river, like life,
is littered with rejected poems, and thick

with poets desperately dog-paddling for the shore.

The Needle

I'd always assumed I'd outlive my dogs,
but at sixty-four realize that's foolishness.

Today, on the way to my doctor's office,
they look at me with weepy, goodbye eyes

yet glare at one another, and I suspect
this rare belligerence stems from a dispute

over the trip home, a squabble over who'll
get to ride up front, and who'll get to drive.

Near McDowell's Farm

While combines raise small whirlwinds
of chaff and dust, we wander the fallow cemetery,
weaving through its stubble of weathered stones.
I'm told a hundred were buried in that corner of
the field, though fewer than thirty markers remain,
the most recent occupant *coming home* in 1946.

But what seizes my attention are
the dates. Many born with the century, died
between the fall of 1918 and the following spring,
victims of the Spanish Flu. A unique plague
in that it spared small children and the elderly
but displayed an insatiable appetite for young adults.

And who could miss the terrible irony
of returning sons, spared by the trenches, bringing
death, an old companion, back to meet family, friends
and neighbours. A deadly virus calling at every
village and farm, making itself at home amidst
a relentless barrage of tolling bells.

In a country where nothing went to waste,
they were buried in the same scrimped-for suits and
dresses made for graduations, weddings, and Armistice Day.
The music of those last dances still echoing
as the old gave their children back to a God who, after
demanding everything else, now demanded this.

Grandfather

With his reputation as a hard drinker,
my grandfather, head librarian at one of England's
prestigious public schools, sipped his tea, saying nothing
as he stared out the Common Room window and watched
a large jaguar cross the far end of the playing field.

Sober enough, that day, to know declaring
such a sighting would invite some wag to respond
that the big cat was probably the Parade Marshal,
soon to be followed by a long line of pink elephants,
bagpipe-playing hippos, and dancing bottles of Guinness.

Half believing that himself, months
later he read with relief The Sunday Times'
reports of gutted cattle found on a dozen far flung
Surrey farms, and grainy photos of sceptical biologists
crouched over huge paw prints along quiet country streams.

The perpetual pint in his right hand, again, steady as a rock.

France 1914

in memory of John Larcombe

My grandfather described that Christmas Eve —
how both sides, after a few tentative gestures,
set aside their weapons and climbed from the trenches
to exchange chocolate and cigarettes.

Many, strolling to nearby villages, filled the cafés,
draining their wine cellars; the same familiar carols
rising in a marriage of English and German until outraged
officers drove them back to their lines.

By dawn, frozen blood, like bright holly berries,
beaded their tunics. Ninety years, and as many million
dead later, it sometimes occurs to me in moments of naivety,
that it all could have ended there,

with screaming officers drowned out, guns
abandoned to the mud and snow, and a dozen
drunken armies, all still singing, staggering home
along the frozen roads.

ESL

They frequently shake their heads,
bury their faces in their hands, frustrated

with the endless multiple meanings
and pronunciations as illogical as any

in Chinese or Welsh. Though they
cheer up considerably when I inform them

that the man who contributed most to the
Oxford English Dictionary, the Bible of the

language, was as mad as a hatter, and
spent most of his life confined to an asylum.

Nuisance Ground

At the nuisance ground the new caretaker
breaks open the bloated, green bags, places
overripe fruit, fish guts, and jam jars along
the edge of the pit, sets a banquet for the
bears that arrive with the moon.

He explains that with the high fire hazard
he can't burn now, that if the goodies remain
bagged they'd simply drag them out, spread
the contents across the hillside, leaving
him to clean up the mess.

But his sheepish grin, and the devotion
brought to the task, suggest it's less a case of
common sense and more a matter of offerings —
a propitiatory act, a bush version of candles
on shrines, virgins into volcanoes.

A more practical approach than that of
his predecessor, a tight-fisted bastard who
gave away nothing, carried a gun yet was badly
mauled twice before torching the whole pit and
driving off in search of more secular employment.

X

Back then we'd joke that our house
must bear some secret mark
announcing to all stray cats and dogs that
they wouldn't be turned away.

As a gypsy patrin, shaped from sticks,
identifies clan and destination,
so, perhaps, behind the flowerbed or the back shed,
there was a small inukshuk constructed of dog turds,

or a dead mouse, its tail a finger pointing
to our worn welcome mat, beyond which
three dogs and seven cats dozed contentedly,
exposing us as easy marks.

Today, those pets now scattered
or dead, I imagine the poems find me
in much the same way: the tiny symbol of a pen
scratched into the brick outside my window,

its nib directing them to the stairwell, at the top
of which they whine and mewl until I open the door;
my one surviving dog, with a sigh of resignation,
sniffing each new piece as it stumbles in.

Doggy Day Care

I picture them
making their way home in the afternoon,

her collar studded with gold stars,
carrying her brilliant, original artwork in her mouth,

while he clumps along far behind,
dawdling as usual, half-digested crayons colouring his drool.

Tomorrow he'll be the genius,
painting a rainbow worthy of Picasso across the snowy yard.

She Found It Funnier Than I Did

On my 63rd birthday
my daughter drove me home after dinner.

As usual, not paying
attention, I climbed from the car before

realizing she'd stopped
a block short, in front of a funeral home.

One can only hope
she displays the same sense of humour

the day they read my will.

English Mother

No matter the disaster — grave illness,
sudden death, broken bones or broken heart —

she puts the kettle on, warms the pot,
absolutely sure in an unsure world that,

though a cup of tea might not put things right,
it is, without doubt, the first step on the road there.

Grace

In our childhood no clenched fist
hammered the Bible for emphasis.
No bellowed proverb preceded the
wooden spoon, and where twisted
Christs decorated neighbours' walls
we stuck up posters of Albert Einstein
and a long succession of astronauts.

Under our roof Newton and Darwin
were as familiar and irrefutable
as the Scriptures elsewhere. At our
table all meals were served heavily
spiced with science, and following each
of my father's booming pronouncements
my brother and I, in lieu of the common 'Amen,'
would reverently mutter $E=MC^2$.

Island

for Rick Simison

Focus on the corner of this floating dock
when waves roll in from the west, and you
can imagine the tip of this island as the prow
of a moving ship — a rocky, pine-covered liner —
slowly steaming past a shoreline where the Stars
and Stripes vie with the Maple Leaf, identifying
the deed holders.

Opened with the building of the Rideau
Canal, the land was gutted by mines, soon
plowed under, and in time transformed into a
sporting ground for the rich — their hunting and
fishing estates now split and parcelled into summer
cottages for great grand-children, the howling of jet
boats replacing the long-eradicated wolf.

This land is too tame, most of it levelled and
subdivided, domesticated by a century of
tourism. A land too soft for those of us more
at home in younger country where great fields
of rock, tilted on edge, promise sudden death
to the careless and unprepared. Where bush and
stone devour survey stakes and short-lived clearings.

So, let's sail the island away, brother,
up through the Rideau Lakes, taking a hard left
at Ottawa, steering north through the Gatineau
Hills and into that great blank space beyond
road maps and navigation charts, in search of
some wilder place in which to anchor, miles
north of neighbours and the last foolish flag.

Tea Ceremony

In memorium, Carol Humphreys

This evening word reaches me
that you're dying in a Regina hospital.

Only months ago, both early risers,
I'd make us tea in the mornings while

the rest of the house, all coffee lovers,
slept in. Strangers thrown together by

the linking of our children's lives,
we carefully weighed then warmed to

one another over strong cups
of Red Rose. Tonight, miles west

of your death, I stay up late
holding a solitary vigil, and make us tea

one last time, mine with milk and
sugar, yours black and unsweetened,

which I'll empty in the morning,
cold and untouched, before washing

and rinsing the cups, before
getting on with this living business

as all who remain behind
must eventually do, one cup at a time.

Dog Years

At fifteen they're prone
to mini-strokes, the vet says.
This, to explain why Max leaps
to his feet several times a night to
growl and bark at some ghostly apparition.

Fifteen. Over a hundred
in dog years. '*Mini-strokes*,' be
damned. He's spotting the same
terrifying shape that often creeps
across the corner of my eye at sixty-three.

Kōan

A single, severed pigeon wing
lying on the sidewalk this morning:
wreckage from a late night, mid-air
collision; the missing pieces of fuselage
probably salvaged by a scavenging cat.

Or possibly a miraculous escape,
I think, glancing at the Buddhist Temple
across the street where I imagine orange-
robed monks, their enlightened ears cocked at the
sky, meditating on the sound of one wing flapping.

Trumpeter Swan

Sailing out of the dark
she dropped anchor off the end of the dock
announcing her arrival with a trumpet blast
loud enough to raise the Baptists from the dead,
and certainly me from my bed.

In honour of that rare,
royal visit, following protocol, I pulled on
my tattered livery of worn jeans and torn
T-shirt, knelt on the rough boards at 2 a.m.,
and served crackers to the queen.

Roll

Three a.m., and the last time I glanced at the clock,
only minutes ago it seems, it wasn't yet eleven.
All night I've worked and reworked this page, altering
a phrase here, deleting a word there, or, in moments
of editorial viciousness, slashing complete lines.

Wearing a trail across the carpet, slippered feet
counting written feet, I pace the piece out, hunting
for just the right rhythm, and pity the other writers
in this town who abandoned their pens hours ago
for warm beds and even warmer lovers.

Who right now are probably shaping flesh with
almost the same enthusiasm with which I shape
this poem. Though some, crawling from disheveled
beds for a cold glass of water or a quick wipe-down,
may glance from their windows

to see my light still burning before shuffling back
to their prosaic beds, cursing their bitter lot in life.

Blowin` Smoke Up Your Own Ass

Afraid of what I`ll learn,
I`ve no desire to delve into
the origins of that peculiar phrase,

but can`t help speculating
on the opportunity presented
were I to master such contortions.

At last, putting poetry
far behind me to make some
real money with the Cirque de Soleil.

Voodoo

An acceptable outlet for divorce rage,
each morning I split wood for an hour
until severed heads lay piled knee-deep
around the bloody chopping block.

Within weeks she developed migraines
and a chronically sore neck. Now, increasingly
crippled, she takes to her bed, while I work my way
up another mountainside,

a long line of logging trucks double-shifting to keep up.

Guide to Saskatchewan Gothic

for Darlene Wright

In the cemetery south of Lumsden,
a headstone records a year of birth
as 1944, and the year of death as 2044,

leaving us to conclude
it's either occupied by a liar or
reserved for a very confident psychic.

Guarding the graves of children,
cherubs, angels and lambs, melting under
a hundred years of rain, assume the shapes of gargoyles,

while a nearby mound, showing
evidence of a recent disinterment, sits
surrounded by thirteen, neatly-spaced garlic bulbs.

Though the townsfolk seem
friendly enough, we recommend visitors
ensure they're well clear of the district by nightfall,

and, despite its quaint Bed & Breakfast
sign, travellers are strongly advised to avoid
the local castle, and its resident Count, at any time of day.

Southerly

Up from the Gulf,
it drops heavy snow
on the hills, dusting fields
to the north, leaving crazed,

landlocked gulls screaming,
wheeling half-a-mile high,
sifting the salt wind, stirring
ancestral memories of seas

they`ve never seen,
or could even imagine.

Dietary Facts

She draws up my diet plan,
excluding most things worth eating.
Banishes salt completely. Cuts sugar
by fifty-percent, thereby staggering the
economies of several Caribbean nations.

Loses me completely in the
new math of dieticians: the complex
addition, subtraction and division of
carbohydrates, fibre, and fats (trans,
saturated, and un). Waves off my protests

over the elimination of butter,
deaf to my argument that I consume
butter for religious reasons, it being a
pillar in the Holy Church of Julia Child,
Our Lady of Perpetual French Cuisine.

Turns a painfully thin, cold
shoulder to me as I point out that Julia
died at the age of ninety-one, probably
while nibbling on a sautéed mushroom
between puffs on her twentieth cigarette

of the day, and, her husband,
who ate every fat-saturated morsel
she ever placed before him, passed at
an impressive ninety-two — a smug, sated
decade older than any dietician I've ever met.

Atavist

At the lakeside camp, the radio
throws weather predictions into
thin air while I calculate the altitude
of crows wheeling high above the trees,
study the blue wedge of sky where the
ridges meet behind me, trace the trail of
sundogs chasing their master over the Purcell Range.

Having relearned the language of
water, stone and sky — here, illiteracy
can be fatal — the radio will be abandoned,
the day foretold in the flight paths of birds,
the intricate dance of wind and waves,
the patterns of small bones shaken and
tossed to the ground between my splayed feet.